A New True Book

THE VIDEO REVOLUTION

By Walter Oleksy

CHILDRENS PRESS ®
CHICAGO

PHOTO CREDITS

Bally Midway Manufacturing Co.—2

The Bettmann Archive—4 (3 photos)

Sony Corporation of America—7, 8, 12, 15 (right), 44

Wide World Photos—11, 15 (left), 35, 41

Journalism Services—30, 38
© Scott Wanner—17, 36
© Paul F. Gero—26

Nawrocki Stock Photo:
© Jim Wright—18
© Robert Lightfoot—28

Cameramann International Ltd.—Cover, 19, 20
(2 photos), 21 (2 photos), 22

Video Vendor—24

Pioneer Corporation—32, 33

Robert A. Walsh—40

Epson America—43

Cover: Girl learning sign language using a videotape

Library of Congress Cataloging-in-Publication Data

Oleksy, Walter G., 1930-
    The video revolution.

    (A New true book)
    Includes index.
    Summary: Examines the history, formats, features,
and uses of video tape records and discusses aspects
such as music videos, video discs, piracy, and
possible future developments.
    1.   Home video systems—Juvenile literature.
2.   Video tape recorders and recording—Juvenile
literature.   [1.   Video tape recorders and recording.
2.   Home video systems]   I.   Title.
TK9960.038   1986   621.388'332   85-30850
ISBN 0-516-01285-1   AACR2

TABLE OF CONTENTS

Piano players provided the music for silent movies, such
as the 1913 comedy shown above. Two scenes from the classic
silent movie, "The Great Train Robbery," are shown below.

THE WONDERFUL WORLD OF VIDEO

First came silent movies, in the early 1900s. Then sound movies, in 1927.

In 1920, the first radio station in the United States, KDKA in Philadelphia, began broadcasting.

In 1945 the first television sets were sold. They had high price tags and small screens.

Television changed the way families got their entertainment and news. Many people stopped going out to movie theaters or listening to the radio. They stayed home and watched television.

Thirty years later another electronic marvel appeared. The "Video Revolution" began in 1975 when Sony Corporation introduced Betamax, the first video recorder for home use.

This modern entertainment center has remote control, stereo sound, a TV, video recorder, and laser disc player.

Soon a second type of VCR (video cassette recorder) was introduced—the VHS format. VHS stands for Video Home System.

VCRs have come a long way in a very short time.

Sony Video 8 recorder

Ten years ago, only a few thousand people owned a VCR. Today about 25 million homes—about one in every four—have a VCR. By 1999, 50 million American homes are expected to have at least one VCR.

WHAT VIDEO RECORDERS DO

The first home VCRs were very simple. They could only record off TV or a video camera and play back up to two or four hours of videotape. Blank tape cost about $20.

Early VCRs could not "freeze" or stop a single frame so it could be studied like a still picture.

They couldn't "scan" a tape for fast-forward or reverse viewing.

The sound was strictly monophonic.

Today's VCRs can do those things and more. They can play six or eight hours of tape. They can freeze a frame and play in slow motion. The sound can be high-quality stereophonic.

VCR FORMATS

There are over one hundred models of VCRs. They range in price from about $200 for a basic model to about $1,400 for the latest stereo machines.

Technician tests sound on stereo VCR

Sony's recently developed lightweight video camera
and recorder sells for about $1,200. This system
uses the 8 millimeter format.

For years, VCRs came in
two basic formats—Beta
and VHS. In 1985, a
third—8-millimeter—was
introduced.

None of the three formats is compatible. That is, Beta tape cannot be played on a VHS machine, or vice versa. Smaller 8-mm tape will record and play back only on an 8-mm VCR.

There isn't much difference between Beta and VHS in quality of picture and sound. Their main difference is that

Beta machines and tapes are smaller than VHS but record only up to five hours. VHS machines record up to eight hours.

So far, the quality of 8-mm video is not quite up to Beta or VHS, but it is being improved.

Some predict that the smaller 8-mm video systems may eventually outsell both Beta and VHS.

Stereo video recorders

A wide-range of video recorders (left) are made in Japan. Sony's small color 8-mm video camera (right) is expected to outsell the larger home movie camera systems.

are becoming more popular as stereo TV increases. Popular music fans also enjoy taping their favorite music videos off cable TV in stereo and playing them back on their stereo VCRs.

VIDEO'S IMPACT

Video already has had a tremendous influence on how we live.

Videotapes give people a wide choice of viewing material. They offer a greater opportunity to select what to watch or to reject what is offered on network or cable TV.

One of the best-liked and most-used features of VCRs is "time-shifting." A VCR's timer device can be

Close-up of a few of the VCR controls

set to record a movie or TV show while the family is out of the house. The tape can be played back later, whenever wanted. The tape can be erased or kept and added to a family's video library.

This professor of speech uses videotapes to help his students improve their presentations.

Many teachers now use VCRs in the classroom. Showing a videotape of a movie or other educational material can visualize a subject to help students learn.

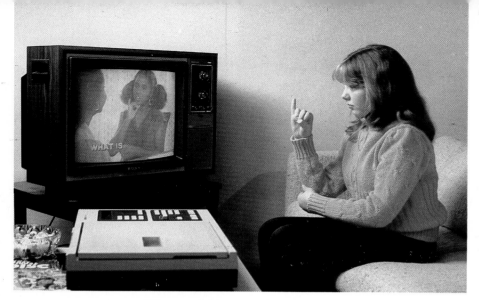

Young girl learns sign language using a videotape.

New stereo broadcasting and monitor TV sets offer bilingual programming and taping. One sound channel can be in English, the other in Spanish or another language. With the flip of a selector switch, one or the other can be chosen.

"How-to" program on origami (above)
and cooking (right)

Bilingual broadcasting and video recording can become important educational tools in the home and school.

There are about fourteen thousand movies and "how-to" programs available to rent or

Shorts 'n Tops Coordinates
Athletic group   Frame #2237
Athletic group   Frame #2364
Mesh Knit group   Frame #2263
NFL group   Frame #2282
Baseball group   Frame #2299
More Shorts
Assortment   Frame #2148
Camp style   Frame #2170
Swim Trunks   Frame #2316
Jeans   Frame #2103
Belts   Frame #2100
More Boys', Teens' Fashions>>>

In some places people can order clothes and other items from a videotape.

purchase on video cassette. Hundreds more are added each month.

People can shop at home by use of their VCR. A tape plays half an hour of commercials. Products are demonstrated. If the

21

Someday video cassettes may replace printed catalogues.

viewer sees anything he or
she wants to buy, a
telephone call and credit
card are all that are
needed to make a purchase.
Some people buy
relaxation tapes. They
show fish swimming in a

tank or scenes of forests and lakes, with soothing music to relax the viewer.

There is even a tape to relax the dog that is left home alone. It's called "Arf!" and contains half an hour of scenes of dogs barking, a quiz show with a dog host and panel, and a dog newscast.

Videotapes can be rented at supermarkets,

department stores, and
video vending machines.

In many homes, the VCR
has brought families closer.
The whole family can
enjoy a video movie for far
less money than it would
cost to go out to a movie
theater.

VIDEO GAMES

Video games played through a TV set and the use of a VCR or computer are not only fun, they can be educational.

Many educators like video games because they can help bring textbook lessons to life.

Action video games also teach dexterity skills.

Before VCR recorders and computers, video games could only be played at machines at arcades and shopping malls.

Players can learn to think and react rapidly while trying to build up a high score by shooting down spaceships in a video game.

Video games were being used with computers in 1962. It wasn't until 1979 that they became widely popular. That was when a Japanese company introduced Americans to "Space Invaders." Four million quarters were spent on the game in video arcades.

Some people say video games create stress and anxiety. Others say they

help a player develop
alertness and hand-eye
coordination.

New video games are
played with special
electronic 3-D glasses.

MUSIC VIDEO

Each year about two thousand four-minute music videos are made and shown over MTV, the all-music cable TV network, and thousands of independent stations around the country.

Like mini-musical movies, they feature the star of a new phonograph recording, usually a rock performer. They promote

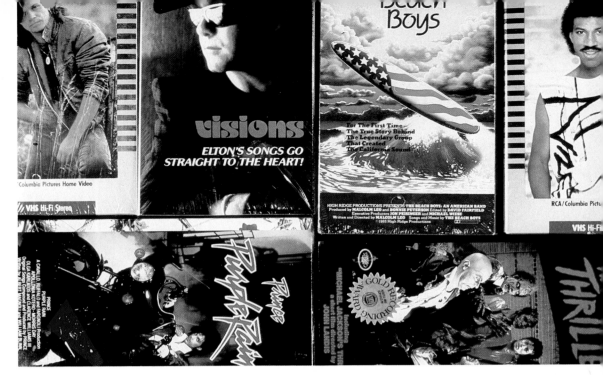

Samples of music videotapes

the star's record and in some cases a full-length motion picture the singer or band has made.

Record companies spend about $100 million a year making music videos.

The average video costs $15,000 to make. Some cost as much as $100,000 if they are big productions such as "Making Michael Jackson's 'Thriller.' "

Rock singer Prince reached superstardom with his video "When Doves Cry," a four-minute preview of his hit movie *Purple Rain.*

Music videos also are sold for about $30, and many fans build large home libraries of their favorites.

VIDEO DISCS

Video discs play both picture and sound on video disc players.

At present there is only one type of video disc recorder being made, the laser disc player. A laser

Video disc

Laser disc players and discs project very clear pictures.

beam reads millions of bits
of picture and sound
information on a disc. The
information is then sent
from the video disc player
onto a TV screen.

Video discs can store
incredible amounts of

material. All the paintings and sculpture of a great museum can be stored on just one disc. A viewer can freeze a frame and study a particular painting for as long as is wanted without damaging disc or machine, since the laser light does not touch the disc to wear it out.

An entire encyclopedia of ten thousand pages with nine million words and

This 12-inch video disc can store the same amount of slides stored in 540 slide trays or information equal to four million words on one side of the disc.

thousands of pictures also can be stored on just one video disc.

New uses of laser discs for science and industry are being discovered regularly.

VIDEO "PIRACY"

People who make copies of movies on videotape and sell them without permission of the makers of the tape are called "video pirates."

Sample of the variety of videotapes available for sale

Those who make electronic boxes that can bring in cable TV stations without paying for them are engaging in video piracy.

Moviemakers who also produce movies on videotape and discs are starting to fight back by "scrambling" the tapes and discs so they can't be copied onto a video recorder. A system called Macrovision uses a special

Sample of videos for children

signal to prevent a tape or
disc from being copied.

More tapes and discs
may be equipped with
such a scrambling device
in the future.

Cable TV networks may
also use such a scrambler
on their broadcast signals

to prevent owners of home video recorders from taping their movies and shows.

The Supreme Court has ruled that it is legal to tape movies and programs off television, whether it is network or cable TV, so long as the tape is for home use only. It is against the law to charge admission to watch a videotape or disc. It also is illegal to copy a movie and sell it.

WARNING

Federal law provides severe civil and criminal penalties for the unauthorized reproduction, distribution or exhibition of copyrighted motion pictures, video tapes or video discs.

Criminal copyright infringement is investigated by the FBI and may constitute a felony with a maximum penalty of up to five years in prison and/or a $250,000 fine.

Most videotapes of movies start with an FBI warning that it is illegal to copy the tape at all, even if only for home use. Many people ignore this and, if they have two VCRs, play the tape on one machine and record it on the other, building a home library of their favorite movies and music videos. The law isn't interested in prosecuting the individual who copies a tape of a movie. It goes after the video pirate who tries to make a business out of copying tapes.

This new video system allows users to show still photographs on a TV screen. It also can make an "instant" photographic print from a video image. The model holds a sample print she made from the screen.

FUTURE OF VIDEO

Video recorders and cameras of tomorrow are likely to be smaller and cost less than they do today. At the same time they will be easier and more fun to use.

More VCRs and cameras will be portable and combined in one unit.

Just as TV sets are being made smaller and smaller, someday VCRs may be as small as a

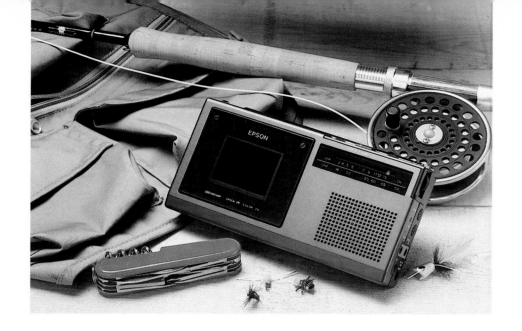

match box. Tapes for them
may be as thin as thread.

These pocket-sized VCRs
may have their own built-in
screens so you can play a
videotape on a bike ride
or at the beach, the way
small TVs and radios can
be played today.

As home TV sets are made with larger screens, VCRs will be made that project clearer pictures that can spread out on the big screens. Sony already has a gigantic 80-by-150-foot TV screen the size of a drive-in movie theater screen, called JumboTRON.

Besides sharper image and better sound, video and TV of the future may be seen in three-dimensions.

Only a little over a decade ago, few people dreamed it would be possible to own a machine that could record and play back movies in the home.

The future of video may hold new marvels no one can even dream of today.

WORDS YOU SHOULD KNOW

Betamax(BAIT • uh • max) — brand name for a format of videotape recorder

bilingual(bi • LING • wal) — able to speak more than one language

cable TV(KAY • bil T • V) — pay-TV transmitted by satellite

computers(kum • PYOO • ters) — electronic information storage devices

copy(KOP • ee) — to reproduce another that is the same as the original

dexterity(DEKS • tair • ih • tee) — skill in using hands or other parts of the body

laser(LAY • zer) — a very powerful, accurate beam of light

laser disc(LAY • zer DISK) — a record read by laser light that can produce both picture and sound

monophonic(mon • eh • FON • ik) — sound with a single output signal

network TV(NET • werk TV) — free TV

revolution(rev • o • LOO • shun) — great change or turning around

scan(SKAN) — quickly look over

"scrambling"(SKRAM • bling) — method of breaking up a TV picture to make it unwatchable

stereo(STAIR • ee • oh) — a sound system producing more than one output signal

Supreme Court(soo • PREEM KORT) — highest court in the United States

"time-shifting"(TYME shift • ing) — recording off TV for later viewing

VCR — video cassette recorder

VHS — Video Home System, a format of video recorder

video "pirates"(VID • ee • oh PIE • ruts) — people who make illegal copies of videotapes or watch cable TV without paying for the service

video recorders(VID • ee • oh ree • KORD • ers) — machines that can record and play back movies and programs off TV

INDEX

About the Author

Walter Oleksy lives in a Chicago suburb and writes books for children and adults. Video is his hobby, and he likes taping movies on his two video recorders and watching movies on his laser disc player. Neighborhood kids like to come to his "home movie theater" and see his movie collection.